An Overview of Strategic Healthcare Marketing

Marketing Mix & Segmentation
Strategies at Work

❧

Dr. Jamie T. Pleasant; Ph.D.

An Overview of Strategic Healthcare Marketing

Marketing Mix & Segmentation
Strategies at Work

&

Dr. Jamie T. Pleasant; Ph.D.

An Overview of Strategic Healthcare Marketing

Marketing Mix & Segmentation Strategies at Work

First Edition / First Printing

ISBN-978-1-940698-00-7

Dedication

To my daddy, Anthony T. Pleasant, who was a perfect example to me of a real man. To Kimberly Pleasant, the love of my life, what a great soul mate you are for me! To my children; Christian Zion and Nacara. I love you all very much!

To all my students at Clark Atlanta University; God bless you!

Humbly Yours in Christ,

Apostle Jamie T. Pleasant

Table of Contents

An Overview of Strategic Healthcare Marketing

This book presents effective ways that healthcare marketing administrators can utilize the marketing mix variables to maximize their delivery of healthcare services. Managed healthcare companies are continuing to look at various ways to develop an effective and efficient brand among many competitors that exists in the healthcare industry. The task of healthcare firms to be the preferred provider for customers over other companies is not an easy undertaking. It requires sound marketing strategies that will establish one healthcare provider's brand over another's. Providers must establish themselves as a brand to compete. As customers are becoming more knowledgeable about healthcare and have more access to databases of all healthcare providers, the ability for a healthcare provider to properly implement the place, price, promotion, and product marketing mix variables will give that firm a sustainable competitive advantage among others. Therefore, healthcare providers must understand and utilize branding strategies based on the marketing mix variables. This book examines each marketing mix variable that a healthcare provider can utilize in order to help establish a credible, unique and powerful brand.

Chapter 1

Product Management Strategies

With the advent of governmental healthcare plans and the changes that increased consumer choices, the health care industry has taken a much needed shift from the traditional ways of providing basic care to consumers. As healthcare costs are continuously rising and providers are forced to consistently find new ways to cut budgets and maximize income, healthcare providers are faced with the challenge of properly managing every asset of their operation in order to be able to compete with government backed insurance plans. At the heart of that, lies the challenge of minimizing costs while maximizing profits within their companies. There is only so much that consumers that need healthcare can afford. As healthcare costs to consumers have continuously increased over the years, the ability to generate healthy revenues for healthcare providers are still lackluster at best. In 2011, the total national health care expenditures rose to 8.9% which is two times the current rate of inflation. Interestingly, in 2012, the per person total spending on healthcare was $2.8 trillion dollars (Munro 2012).

Notably, medical expenditures have increased every year over the past few years. Medical expenditures approximately doubled over the 20 year period from 1959 to 1979 climbing from a little more than 5 percent to 10 percent of personal income. Then during a period of between 1979 to 1994 medical expenditures climbed from 10 percent to 15.6 percent of personal income. The decline in the personal savings rate was very pronounced beginning in the mid 1980s as medical expenditures climbed from 12 percent to almost 16 percent of personal income. In 2012, employer insurance premiums are two and half times the rate of current inflation at 5.0%.

While product management as it pertains to healthcare has several aspects, this book will focus on product line management and product development and modification as two areas which significantly impact the provision of health care. Product line management has become more important to health care providers as the competitive market place has driven some providers to specialize and differentiate their services offered. As cost reductions become pinnacle to bottom line success for hospitals, product line management has inevitably become an important concept of practice in the health care industry. France and Glover (1992) offer a framework that consists of utilizing a *bundle-of-elements* concept for defining product line management (PLM) as having the ability to (1) increase perceptions of quality (2) position the product for specific segments, (3) overcome erratic demand in the health care environment, and (4) reduce nonmonetary costs for health care consumers. It is this *"bundle-of-elements"* concept that help hospitals create several products and services from the same set of existing elements of their offerings to be further developed producing and variations of the product or service to differentiated market segments. It is these variants that offer hospitals the ability to control costs and reach specific target markets with precision.

Nadiu, Kleimenhagen & Pillari (1993) suggests that there are certain circumstances that (PLM) is likely to be most successful. PLM is suggested as being most effective as a management tool for hospitals that comprise the following characteristics: (1) at least medium size, (2) located in a highly competitive area serving at least 200,000 or more people, (3) the populated area must demonstrate a marketing orientation and finally, (4) features areas of excellence in their product mix offerings to the public. Overall the biggest impact that PLM has for health care providers like hospitals is that of positive bottom line results. If a hospital fits the above profile, PLM is recommended (Gorchels 1995). Product management teams are being formed among hospitals as they begin to place a manager over certain areas of a hospital to coordinate the daily

17

functions of business. Grayson (1994) illustrates the fact that hospitals are adapting to PLM concept as they have begun to consolidate health care providers.

Malhotra (1986b) defines product portfolio as the ability of firms to develop strategic program units (SPUs) that better describes specialized aspects of products offered to a clearly defined market and requires its own distinct program strategy. With product mix strategies that tie into product line management and development, hospitals and other health care providers must determine the appropriate mix of products and the markets that they are to serve.

Kenkel (1993) shows how mergers help companies set up SPUs that strategically place them into markets that will increase their competitive advantage and profitability. As managed care continues to increase its presence in health care, mergers and acquisitions have become an industry norm in order to purchase business units that can help diversify a health care firm's product offerings in an environment that fosters choices to consumers that demand various product offerings. Columbia health care Corporation and HCA hospital Corporation of America merged and demonstrated that they clearly wanted to increase their efficiency in operations and offer better patient care (Modern Healthcare 1993). The merger positioned both the company as a multi health care provider and they were able to fill various niches that they could not address before. As a result of the merger, they created a hospital system that now generates over $10 billion dollars in yearly revenues.

19

Chapter 2

Product Development and Modifications

Product development is essential in the product life cycle that exists for any given product category. The health care industry is no exception to constant change of consumer needs, motives and services that they expect to receive. West (1995) shows how Clinch Valley Medical Center reorganized its laboratory to make it more efficient and provide new (ER) service delivery to patients. Consumers mentioned that they desired the ability to get quality efficient care in emergency room treatment situations at all times, which was sparse in health care facilities across the country. As a result of these consumer expressed needs, the hospital developed new services for emergency room that decreased treatment turnaround time by utilizing and relocating a underused satellite laboratory to the emergency room area. They further developed expedient ways of treating emergency room patients by restructuring the way phlebotomists perform their work. Phlebotomists began to perform their services on hospital floors, which decreased their turnaround time with patients significantly. This new delivery of service to customers, provided better consumer ratings of its emergency room service and revenues increased for the hospital, while costs were greatly reduced.

As managed care continues to grow in the health care industry, hospitals and other providers must develop new services and products.. Greene

(1995) illustrates how Spectrum Health care Services (an emergency treatment firm) teamed up with four hospitals in 1994 to offer emergency medical service to managed care providers. This partnership with hospitals has worked well with many managed care providers as this is the only way they can compete with the increased desire of consumers to belong to managed care health plans. This new product development that forms a portfolio of separate health care services have combined to provide revenues that could never be realized before the partnership.

Hospitals have even begun to develop new services to reach underserved communities that most health care providers have shunned (Taylor 1993). Elliot Hospital and Catholic Medical Center in New Hampshire teamed up to provide better care to medically underserved communities. Interestingly, the process significantly reduced operation costs. They even formed a project that organized a clinic that targets uninsured and underinsured patients who formally used emergency rooms as their only place to receive health care. As the need to develop these new services continue to increase, the companies that are adapting and responding to a changing environment are seeing revenues increased significantly as they reach a heavily populated market segment that has no place to go to receive health care.

Chapter3

Pricing Strategies

In order to provide effective and efficient health care, important elements of pricing include competitive pricing strategies, price discrimination, and efficient pricing and billing systems. In the eighties (80s), for profit hospitals had policies of charging as much as the market would bear for particular services rendered. Patients were charged for equipment and supplies on an itemized basis. As managed care entered into the market, hospitals have been forced to reduce their pricing structures to remain competitive in a turbulent health care environment that stresses cost reductions and quality of care. Nemes (1993) shows how for-profit hospitals are changing their pricing practices and strategies as managed care and fixed reimbursements become the focal point of the health care industry. Even after lowering their prices, for-profit hospitals still have gross charges that are 11% higher than those for tax-exempt hospitals. Hospitals like Human Inc. are seeking to lower their prices further by improving relations with physicians after adversarial past histories.

With the advent of the Prospective Payment System (PPS), the reimbursement of hospital costs based on pre-calculated set prices rather than on the costs actually incurred by each patient will drive prices down for health care services. The PPS has successfully boosted economic competitive conditions between hospitals participating in the Medicare program. The PPS has been attributed to producing equilibrium pricing that has for so long, influenced insurance companies payment schemes that also increased health care prices.

Health Insurance Purchasing Cooperatives (HIPCs) are also playing an important part in reducing the price of services rendered by health care firms. Some states across the country are beginning to use HIPCs to implement the principles of managed competition to solve coverage problems while maintaining consumer choice and controlling price and quality of services provided (Blankeau 1993). As managed care's presence increases and cost reductions continues as a major focus of health care organizations, prices will be reduced and passed on to consumers as the health care providers become more efficient in delivery of their services.

As managed care and other forms of health care continue to increase their presence in the industry, price negotiations for contracts among hospitals, medical centers and managed care firms are significantly changing. Malhotra (1996) shows how a medical center in Denver Colorado develop several computer simulation models on costs and profitability that formed optimal contract bidding prices that were to be presented to managed care organizations. As a result of providing such promising data, the medical center won 42 contracts with managed care organizations in 18 months.

Price discrimination has long been a practice in all aspects of a given industry. The

28

ability for a firm to charge different rates for the same level of service at different times or economic environment conditions are key factors that exist in a competitive market place. The story remains the same for health care providers as they discriminate their prices based on market conditions. Rosk (1994) illustrates how hospitals have practiced cost shifting by charging different amounts for the same services to private patients not covered by Medicare or Medicaid have proven to be good business practices. A survey of 201 Pennsylvania hospitals analyzed markups based on severity of illness, type of coverage the patient had and cost of treatment based on diagnosis related groups (DRGs). The study concluded that hospitals find that price discrimination is necessary to remain competitive in a managed care environment.

Hospitals have been aware of their billing procedures and a lack of cost and quality control for many years. Competition has finally forced them to develop better ways to manage and be accountable for daily transactions and billing procedures. Anderson and Johnson (1992) examine the fact that hospitals have created a confusing billing and pricing system that is causing a large amount of customer dissatisfaction. They further show how consumer confusion would lesson if hospitals would streamline their charge structures, explain to businesses the complex reasons for cost shifting and keep prices in line with costs. Billing procedure improvements and collection service revision would significantly improve their cost structures and thus would result in savings to consumers as prices for various services would decrease.

30

Chapter 4

Promotional Strategies

Advertising, that in the past focused on scare tactics to lure consumers into hospitals and other forms of care, now employs specialized messages with emphases on particular programs and services that reach a particular segment of the health care market (Denitto 1994). As the health care industry becomes more segmented and competitive, advertising messages must become more innovative and tailored to communicate to specific target markets and their needs that exists (Sturm 1988). Hospitals and other health care providers must develop advertisements that position them as a preferred provider for a particular medical service in order to communicate their uniqueness and distinctiveness in a competitive market place.

31

For example, some hospitals now advertise as being the outpatient specialists, eye surgery experts, trauma care specialists, cancer experts, pediatric care specialists or trauma experts etc. Rabinowitz (1992) shows how The Henrietta Egelston Hospital for children in Atlanta, Georgia has developed a safety ad campaign that features light-hearted commercials directed by Steve Colby. He made the use of bright, primary colors to attract the attention of both adult and children to associate the hospital with the spots. The campaign is currently featuring a range of dangers such as leaving infants alone in bathtubs and crossing the street without looking in both directions. As result of this, Egelston Hospital continues to be the preferred health care provider of children in the Atlanta market. By carving niches for specialized care, through competitive positioning, advertising has played its role in reducing the cost of hospital care and increasing the efficiency of health care (Raphael 1993).

The influence of perceptual and demographic factors on consumer dispositions in the 90s are of the utmost importance in hospital advertisements. Research now shows that consumers either perceive advertisements of hospitals as favorable or unfavorable based on attitude formation as ad portrayals are viewed. Andaleeb (1994) shows how perception and attitude development are key elements in a viewer's mind as to whether or not a health care ad is found favorable or non favorable in ad test studies. As hospitals develop advertisements, demographic and psychographic variables must be included to develop advertisement portrayals that are favorable with diverse consumer groups.

Traditional business advertisements are also produced with the notion of increasing or establishing an image about a particular product in the market. Public image is very important for hospitals as they are very salient entities in a community and must be able to capitalize on key attributes that consumers are looking for that go beyond the delivery of health care. Perry (1991) shows how the consumer wants to be made aware of the level of community involvement that the hospitals have. Perry (1989) examines the importance of image advertising, as Memorial Health Inc. spent $2 million dollars on an ad campaign to tout their new image. After several weeks, increased consumer confidence and company revenues were experienced.

Infomercials are other alternative forms of advertisements that take a health care provider's services and present them in 30 minutes or a longer format without commercial interruptions. These informative advertisement tactics has proven successful for various products across different categories in the business world. Infomercials are now in the experimental stage as better means of reaching specialized consumers of health care. Gattuso (1994) shows how St. Judes Children's Hospital in Memphis, Tennessee has developed such specialized advertisements to focus in on children that are primary users of their service with John Goodman and Marlo Thomas as spokespersons that children can identify with.

These infomercials are shown on television channels that are frequently watched by children and parents at peak viewing times for their specialized audience.

Direct marketing as a promotion tool has increased industry wide and is a cost efficient way to target customers. Direct marketing is employed by many health care professionals to further enhance image and goodwill (Peltier 1994). Many hospitals today are bypassing traditional advertising in favor of direct marketing strategies. 87% of hospitals have used direct marketing within the last year and 56% have increased their direct marketing budget over the past three years (Kleimenhagen and Pillari1994). The major advantages behind direct marketing include the following: (1) increased response rates that are measurable, (2) targets a desired specialized market versus a mass audience, (3) enables marketers to personalize messages, and (4) develop proprietary databases that are accessible and can be updated with ease and reduced added costs. As health care becomes more segmented and cost efficient, health care professionals will begin to target their treatment areas and narrow their databases in order to reach desired patients and health care users.

Jensen (1989) shows how direct mail has become the primary and preferred source of health care information for consumers. She further illustrates how research presents the fact that recall for health care messages sent by direct mail were significantly higher versus other forms of media. Direct mail offers unique opportunities for health care providers to effectively communicate their product and service offerings and simultaneously develop databases that can help them reach consumers that they are targeting.

Other promotion tools that are used by health care professionals include hospitals that distribute coupons to patients. Promotions go beyond coupon drops and direct mail. Public relations and fund raising projects are pinnacle events that health care providers must employ in a competitive marketplace. The ability to develop goodwill and consumer confidence are at the heart of every marketing and business activity. However, the health care industry is trying to find the proper place and mix for public relation PR activities. Most hospitals have all but abandoned this activity because of the time and effort requirements that are placed on staff and administrators. As the debate and level of importance of PR managers versus fund raising managers increase as it relates to hospital revenues, the levels of goodwill, consumer confidence and trust are still being jeopardized.

Health care servicers are also converting from traditional "fixer-upper" centers to "preventive-wellness" promotion programs (Johnson 1992). Medical prevention and wellness programs organized by hospitals are effective at educating consumers on health topics and have been proven to generate goodwill for medical institutions. Surprisingly, medical institutions have found that these wellness or preventive programs have not alienated physicians and their support .

The promotion of health care goes beyond the efforts of providers. Corporations in America are promoting wellness programs in order to help reduce their costs of medical insurance requirements. Stout (1991) shows how paying workers for good habits catches on as a way to cut medical costs. The economic aspects of wellness programs provide immeasurable ways of reducing costs by increasing moral and motivation of employees, developing goodwill between employee and employer and reduced the number of sick days in the work place. Wellness programs have been shown to reduce the need for health care (Templin 1990). Johnson and Johnson Incorporated shows how their wellness programs help substantially reduce the cost of health care over years.

Chapter 5

Place Management And
Distribution Strategies

Earlier in the book we have documented the growing trend toward managed care. Here, such systems for delivering health care are discussed in more detail along with the traditional channels. We also discuss the location of medical services. HMOs (health maintenance organizations) are the strictest and most inexpensive form of managed care that exists in the marketplace today (Investors Business Daily 1995). HMOs are organized into four types: group practice model, individual practice association (IPA) model, staff model, and network model. In the group practice model, a health plan pays a medical group for contracted service at a negotiated rate. That group is responsible for compensating its physicians and contracting with hospitals for care of their patients. IPA is a health care model that contracts with an entity, which in turn contracts with physicians, to provide health care services in return for a negotiated fee. Physicians continue their existing individual or group practices and are compensated on a per capita, fee schedule, or fee-for-service basis. In the staff model, an HMO employs physicians to provide health care to its members. All premiums and other revenues accrue to the HMO, which compensates physicians by salary and incentive programs. In the network model, an HMO contracts with a network of medical groups.

HMOs provide a reduction of costs for the consumer with the added confidence that the level of care is precise and not wasteful. This segment of health care is conducive and comprised of the health-conscious and thrifty consumers that are tired of being over-charged for unnecessary care. This segment is very appealing to corporate America as it is the lowest cost form of care that boasts and rewards preventive health care. Preferred provider organizations (PPOs) can be arranged through insured or self funded plans. A contract is established with various providers of medical care where there is a benefit contract that provides significantly better benefits (fewer copayments) for services rendered by preferred providers. This discourages the use of non provider care by the consumer. If however, the consumer wants to go to a non-provider, he will pay for the care on traditional "fee-for-service" plans.

In this form of health care delivery, consumers are given more choices and thus PPOs are referred as "choice friendly" forms of managed care. However, with an increase in choices, the increase in cost of care also occurs. Notably, the fact that costs are greater for PPOs versus HMOs, they are still a lot lower than traditional indemnity plans (Investors Daily 1995). With the increase in consumer choice for various levels of care, PPOs have served and identified with a market that has boasted a share of the strongest growth in managed care forms (Investors Daily 1995). This growth is due to the fact that consumers can save on medical costs without giving up on options of the form of care that can be received based on their choice of care. This segment of consumers don't mind paying the extra money for the care they feel they need with the person that they are confident with

44

and have developed trust in. This is one of the major differences between an HMO and a PPO. To these consumers, trust, confidence and options are worth the extra costs.

Point-Of Service-Plans (POSPs) allow the covered person to choose to receive a service from participating or non-participating providers under the direction of a doctor, with different benefit levels associated with the use of participating providers. Actuary services are included to establish probabilities of different levels of care needed by consumers. Doctors create and form a network with POS doctors that become locked in the network to provide care for the consumer. However, this is the most expensive form of managed care to date. The expensive nature of this managed care vehicle comes from the fact that 3rd party carriers and doctors form a network that reduces consumer anxiety about managed care and further establishes their relationships with traditional doctors and insurance companies.

This segment is doctor driven and identifies with consumers who believe that the doctor knows bests (traditional care system) and goes to the doctor to receive direction on the next step of care that must be provided. The doctor serves as an expert, anxiety reducer and traditional figure along with a little touch of cost cutting that comes from managed care. While this form of managed care is the highest cost to consumers, it reaches a segment of the market that is risk averse when it comes to new levels and forms of health care. The consumer in this segment is open to options where security and tradition are important factors in the medicating process. The doctor is the dominate figure here, where relationship and the security of an insurance carrier increase the trust of the consumer in this form of managed care. This segmentation structure is supported by the fact that POSPs shared the lead in growth of consumer markets in managed care (Investors Daily 1995).

Traditional doctors and the way they are trained, conduct business and are hired by hospitals have changed dramatically. Traditional care focused on doctors that were specialist and had been trained as specialists to fill certain needs of a given hospital and patients (Eckholm 1995). The hospital, doctor and 3rd party insurer operated separately in the development of health care packages and plans for patients. As a result, doctors began to specialize as hospitals required them to focus on one field of research and medical service. The traditional doctor only saw certain types of patients and charged them a premium because the customer base was sparse. As a result of doing this, costs for medical services increased significantly over the past years and health care wastes continued to add up. Traditional doctors now are faced with finding a place as HMOs and other managed care programs come into existence. Primary care physicians will be in demand in the future as they direct the level of care that a patient will need, in an effort to minimize cost and maximize efficiency and effectiveness. Schwartz and Steckler (1995) state that the wave of the future is with HMOs and primary care doctors and there is no way that anyone one can stop them.

While traditional doctors are still needed, their importance will diminish as the industry looks at ways to reduce costs and increase efficiency. Specialist will have to retrain (which will be difficult) to primary care in order to survive the managed care wave (Rosenthal 1995). Rosenthal (1995) further reports that in 1995 there has been a remarkable upswing in the number of med-school students seeking training in primary care fields like family practice, internal medicine and pediatrics, and a decline in the previously popular field specializations. In the New York area where doctors once regarded contractual arrangements with HMOs as a deal with the devil, now they have begun to form physician networks that give them more leveraging power when negotiating (Rosenthal 1995). Traditional recruitment of physicians were based on specialization and the need of doctors to fill a certain spot. Today, direct recruitment of physicians are conducted by managed care organizations such as HMOs where the doctor is offered a certain amount of money to work at their facility for a certain number of hours per week. This direct recruitment with a decrease in bookwork and medical staffing problems that came with private practice, has lured many physicians to HMOs and other managed care networks Miller (1995). Managed care attracts physicians who will not have to worry about adding to their high leveraged debt ratio with student loans and loans that would be required to open and operate a private practice. As services and methods of services are becoming more segmented, doctors are being recruited more directly by hospitals and managed care organizations in order to respond to the changing health care environment. Incentives and bonuses for primary care physicians are being touted as the way to directly recruit these physicians that will service health care in the 21st century.

As in all markets, a company may have the best products, services and staff in an industry but the consumer may not have access to the company. If this is the case, full market potential may not be reached as segmented markets and other areas of coverage are not properly serviced. Guseman (1988) shows how hospitals are losing out to medical centers based on their ability to adapt to demographic trends and fill niches in areas where service wasn't once offered. The industry is recognizing that with unique and specialized customers, medical services must be available at their place of need. Medical centers and emergency centers (EC) are now being located in convenient places in order to provide medical services that are needed. As a result of past rural areas being undeserved and underrepresented by health care business, some health care organizations have begun to target them as the next growth area to open up medical centers and free standing centers. Lau (1995) illustrates how Medical Control Inc., a new and upcoming PPO, has targeted rural areas versus other PPOs. Medical Control Inc. is targeting non-urban niches and cashing in on their ability to deliver a service to a once deprived community. Medical Control Inc. has shown that customers have continuously appreciated their service in these areas by increasing their participation in the program on all levels. Lau (1995) goes on to add that health care coverage by corporations have been so strongly attracted to Medical Control's programs because they fill a need that has existed for a long time. That need is that corporations don't just need coverage in urban areas, they need it in all the areas their employees will work or live.

As a result of the rural explosion for health care needs, Medi-Centers are cropping up all over remote areas of the country. They are being strategically placed in suburbs where once there weren't enough medical centers located within comfortable distances to consumers in case of emergencies. These centers provide less intensive care versus hospitals and therefore reduce costs for the consumer and the hospital. Hospitals are also branching their services across remote areas of the country as they compete with Medi-Centers that are strategically placed across the country. It is advantageous for hospitals to branch in order to remain competitive and adapt to the change that is going on in the industry to reduce costs and become more segmented in order to increase efficiency by reaching consumers in all geographic areas.

Chapter 6

Marketing Research and CRM

An aging population, "choice-friendly " providers of care, diverse levels of care needed, ethnic influx of patients, slowed population growth and changing consumer demands for health care leads to marketing research as the only way to properly identify and target diverse consumers and their preferences (Thomas 1993). However, the industry's reaction to these changes in the 1980s did not incorporate marketing research and its ability to achieve and establish segmentation as a means to better serve a changing market place. Added to these conditions, effective ways of reaching a diverse customer base had to be implemented. Health care organizations turned to alternative forms of marketing in response to the inevitable failure of campaigns that employed traditional marketing media as television, newsbooks and billboards without regard for increased marketing research and the impact that could be benefited in the industry

The newer ways of reaching health care consumers for research purposes include, direct mail through informational services and other information system (IS) programs. Thomas (1993) illustrates how database marketing has been dubbed as having the most significant impact on long-term relationships between hospitals and patients as consumer profiles are now being kept and patients are being reminded of schedules of visits and care directly through IS programs. If there are proposed changes in services offered by hospitals, they now can try out their new programs on selected patients through ISs and monitor the responses and adjust strategies that match with preferences in the market place.

Marketing research has seen its growth and importance through the advent of managed care organizations such as HMOs and PPOs. As some managed care organizations become more consumer focused and choice driven, measurements of satisfaction of these various services provided must be assessed. Information systems (IS) provide measurable ways to obtain the information needed in order to measure various aspects of services provided by health care servicers. It is becoming apparent that IS are inevitable as health care providers measure cost and satisfaction levels of patients.

Bazzoli (1993) shows how a community medical center in New Jersey used IS programs to analyze ways to improve their patient's level of satisfaction with emergency room service. Their fear was that if a patient wasn't happy with emergency room service, they would tell at least 10 other people and the effects of bad publicity could be devastating and as a result, significantly reduce revenues. As a result of an assisted IS program and marketing research, patient satisfaction increased from 87% to 98% and staff turnaround decreased from 5% to 2% per year. The center also started continuous quality improvement process' which used staff to implement improvements throughout the facility that was recorded and stored on IS programs.

Some health care servicers have employed ISs that are called Doc-On-A-Disk, that allows the patient to electronically enter their symptom on the computer and a level of care is immediately suggested (Goodwin 1994)). The consumer then waits to see a doctor who now can more quickly prescribe medication based on the computer printout. These ISs greatly reduce the amount of time wasted in the waiting rooms and increase the effectiveness of the doctor by allowing him/her to maximize patient coverage. HMOs and PPOs utilized IS in order that they can provide precise tailored medical services to patients at quality levels. IS help them evaluate doctors as they have varying rate scales for services rendered.

Flanagan (1988) examines the chances of survival and profitability of hospitals in the future as well as their ability to control costs and increase accountability of services rendered. ISs are capable of providing hospitals with general patient care benefits. Strategic marketing ISs are available to hospitals that will help them lower costs and increase efficiency. Intracorp, a company that audits hospital bills over $5000 dollars for insurance companies, finds problems with 90% of the bills it audits. Layers of wastes are found in procedures performed and the ability to line item expenses that are listed. Hospitals are leery of implementing these programs because of political issues surrounding physicians and salaries. However, as managed care continues to dominate health care, cost effective measurements will be expected at all levels and the use of ISs along with market research programs will inevitably increase.

ISs further advance the industry in personalizing services to consumers. Databases are created that remind the consumers of appointments, checkups and suggestions for visitations. They are also being used to mail out direct marketing programs of interest to specific needs of the market (Bazzoli 1993). Database programs are being utilized currently that can help health care servicers predict demand for a certain service and the optimal working time on the patient as it relates to the cost of the procedure. These IS programs are good ways to increase the efficiency of physicians and reduce the costs of health care in the future.

As the healthcare industry becomes more competitive, providers that can maximize the marketing mix variables effectively and efficiently will see their brands preferred by consumers in record numbers. Healthcare consumers want to be able to know what one provider does better than another. Therefore, branding on the marketing mix variables is a great strategy to utilize. One of the competitive advantages that Kaiser Permanente still holds over many healthcare providers in the southeast is their ability to brand and utilize the place variable. In many southeastern metropolitan states, one is prone to see as many Kaiser healthcare facilities as malls and some fast food restaurant chains. Kaiser evens strategically places their healthcare facilities directly off of interstates so that they are visible and easy to get to. Kaiser further utilizes the marketing mix variables with radio and television advertisements. They spend $40 million dollars a year on advertisements to create an awareness about their brand (Kaiser Permanente 2004). They have further branded themselves by communicating in those ads, the theme, "Thrive" stating what they do differently from other health care providers. They have effectively tapped into the current health conscious consumers by developing website offering alternative health solutions, meditation techniques and positive mental exercises. As a result, they have seen a decline in disenrollment of their consumers that they experienced at a record level in 2009.

Chapter 7

Segmentation

Healthcare costs are continuously rising and families are consistently finding ways to cut back on other expenditures in order to afford proper care. The Democrats (who once controlled Congress), and the Republicans (who now control Congress) talked about an uncontrollable "health care crisis" that exits. Is this just political rhetoric, or in fact is the United States experiencing a health care crisis? Unfortunately, even a casual study of medical costs and expenditures suggests that our economy is facing a medical cost crisis that if not corrected could cause a continued stagnation of the U.S. economy.

There are three basic reasons why real medical expenditures are growing so fast in relation to personal income and gross national output. One is that the cost of medical services has been growing very rapidly and the other is that we as a society are consuming more medical services. First we will examine what has happened to the cost of medical services. There has been an alarming increase in simply the cost of medical care during the 80s and 90s.

The second factor that has contributed to soaring medical costs is that we are consuming more medical services. In general, the public consumed more medical services and this has contributed to the average life span increasing from 70.8 years in 1970 to 77.9 years in 2012 with projections to increase to 79 years by 2014 (US

Census). However, the consumption of medical services has been rapidly growing due to the aging of the population. The population ages 65 and over has increased from 8.5 percent of the population in 1950, to 9.8 percent in 1970, to 12.4 percent in 1990, and to a projected 16.5 percent in 2012 (US Census 2011). The elderly have more medical problems. That is why Medicare expenditures are projected to increase by at least 9 percent a year for several years to come.

The third factor is that the health care industry must become both more effective (provide medical services that meet needs) and efficient (improve productivity and reduce costs). The industry is changing and adopting a competitive model that provides the level of service appropriate for the seriousness of the medical problems. To this point it would appear that we can't declare a victory for unleashing competitive forces in the health care industry. However, it does appear that the new medical delivery systems hold promise for the future. The problem of increasing medical cost appears to be related to the fact that the medical changes are not yet pervasive enough to stop the upward spiral of medical cost. The elderly and poor account for almost half of our medical expenditures and new medical delivery systems need to be devised to provide the appropriate level of medical care at lower costs. Until this is done, the benefits of the new managed care medical system are not going to be able to keep medical costs in the United States from growing still larger in relation to income and gross national product.

In this book we propose a marketing orientation approach to meeting the challenge of increasing the effectiveness and efficiency of health care. This calls for developing several segmentation strategies and alternate forms of health care delivery such as managed care, and marketing research and information systems aimed at identifying and satisfying customer needs. Each of these elements of marketing are discussed in detail.

Chapter 8

Generic Segmentation Strategies

Healthcare providers can no longer look at their industry homogeneously as "people that are sick and need care." Unique illnesses require unique attention and treatment techniques and facilities that cater to those unique illnesses will prove profitable and sustain a competitive advantage in a dynamic marketplace. The "one stop shop" for taking care of healthcare issues are long gone in the American culture. Primary care doctors now serve as the beginning person that a patient will see when ill (Kaiser 2008). The primary doctor may first see a patient that is ill and then refer him/her to a specialist to handle the health issue. Another way to look at this procedure of specializing in the diagnosing illnesses and treatment procedures is segmentation. Segmentation is a popular marketing strategy that calls for the division of the total market into smaller, homogeneous segments. This is the same as a doctor evaluating an illness and separating it into a unique classification where adequate care and treatment is given to a patient efficiently and effectively. This lowers overall costs and time for healthcare providers as they can specialize in treatment at the correct facility that can treat the illness. Furthermore, segmentation strategies allows healthcare firms to focus on underserved and overlooked markets that others might not deem important. Marketing programs are then developed and tailored to the needs of each segment (Malhotra, 1986a, 1988). This prevents the fallacy of introducing a single product to a mass market that doesn't utilize the product.

Efficiencies are realized as healthcare providers become more focused on customer needs and can provide services more quickly and accurately. Based on the type of unique medical care required by patients in the 21st century, the health care industry can be segmented as follows: (1) Basic medical care, (2) Hospital stay care, (3) Outpatient care (4) Nursing Home care, (5) Urgent care, (6) In-Home care and (7) Hospice care.

With the advent of the new governmental healthcare system and its changes that increased consumer choices, the health care industry has taken a much needed shift from the traditional ways of providing basic care to consumers. The traditional health care system (indemnity plans) where 3rd party insurers, physicians and hospitals combined forces to provide basic care for consumers on a *"fee-for-service"* , basis are taking a back seat to managed care programs that focus on increased efficiency and effectiveness of health care with choice of coverage for consumers (Miller 1995). The traditional health care system promoted the use of increased procedures performed by doctors that yielded increased earnings. Additionally, these practices drove health care costs up significantly without the concern for cost effectiveness, quality and efficiency of care. As a result, hospitals, insurers and physicians were prospering at the expense of the *"overcared-for"* and *"overprovided-for"* consumer. Merline (1995) shows that traditional "fee-for-service" insurance plans have encouraged so much waste and inefficiencies that eliminating this type of care alone would produce tremendous savings in the entire industry.

Hospitals joined in with 3rd party insurers and physicians in driving up health care costs by prescribing unnecessary overnight stays and procedures that could have been assigned on an outpatient basis and would have saved significant health care dollars (Myerson 1995). As a result of excessive health care provision, Medicare and Medicaid costs increased significantly. As Medicare and Medicaid costs increased, government could no longer support the habits of an industry that disregarded efficiency and effectiveness of health care.

An alternative to traditional health care industry practices and increasing costs led to the utilization of managed care providers (HMOs, PPOs and POSPs). These managed care providers allow the consumer to effectively and efficiently match their health care requirements with the optimal level of care needed. Thus, there is a reduction in health care costs while the quality of service is increased. Managed care has helped lower health care costs for corporations and consumers. Membership in HMOs grew significantly (over 100%) from 25.7 million in 1986 to an estimated 56.0 million members in 1995. From 1995 to 2009 HMO enrollments have increased 42.1% (U.S. Census 2012). In 2012, there were 439 Million people enrolled in HMO plans (MCOL research). The industry has clearly embraced the savings, choices, efficiency and quality of care that managed care provides. It follows that with this increased focus of the industry to meet different levels of consumer health care needs, segmentation strategies must be developed and implemented in the industry, if

76

health providers and servicers are to remain competitive.

Hospitals no longer can be all things to all people. In order to cut costs and remain competitive in a managed care environment, hospitals are being forced to specialize in order to sustain a competitive advantage Schlossberg (1990). The "Health care Financial Management" President, Richard Clarke, believes that given the competitive nature of the health care industry, there are only two routes of survival for hospitals in the 1990s that include: (1) diversification and (2) specialization. Specialization is viewed as a way to trim product line offers and increase efficiency as hospitals compete in a managed care industry.

As a result, hospitals are beginning to position themselves as specialists in certain areas. This helps the consumer to distinguish the types of services that a given hospital is noted for. Egleston Hospital in Atlanta is known as the children experts, St. Judes hospital in Memphis Tennessee is known as the Adolescent cancer care providers, Charter Hospitals nationwide are known for their substance abuse expertise, Grady Memorial Hospital in Atlanta Georgia is known as the trauma experts and Emory University Hospital in Atlanta Georgia is known as the cardio-vascular experts. These special areas of services help the providers to carve a niche positioning. As hospitals gear up for specialization, market segmentation will become a driving thrust behind their sustainability.

Farley (1990) shows how free standing independent hospitals or urgent care centers are becoming more apparent as hospitals compete to win managed care customers. This special branching has proven successful as hospitals have begun to have the ability to segment the health care market and capitalize on changing demographics and patient needs (Garious 1993). OB clinics have proven successful for some hospitals as they have been able to direct care to patients in certain areas where they can get to the place of care efficiently without hassles.

Receiving the proper level of care in an efficient manner creates another segment in the health care industry that needs outpatient services. The outpatient segment of the health care industry has two components that include: (1) satellite

79

branching and (2) free standing centers. Lumsdon (1992) shows how increasing ambulatory care have begun to accommodate the outpatient needs of consumers. Many patients are now automatically by-passing hospitals and going to outpatient centers for care. The care is cheaper and more time effective. Lumsdon (1992) shows that the number of ambulatory care centers grew more than 21% a year from 1984 to 1990 and non-hospital outpatient diagnostic imaging centers performed 32% of the total surgery procedures in 1990. This growth shows that there is a strong segment in the market that requires immediate outpatient care with the ability for a patient to walk in and walk out even after surgery.

Satellite programs are now being established by hospitals along with other health care officials to cater to the increased use of outpatient services by consumers. Satellite centers help hospitals branch into areas of the community accessible to consumers that need care. Satellite programs, also known as networks, provide hospitals and physicians and other health care entities the ability to combat free standing centers that have significantly put a dent in the health care market. Anderson (1992) contends that many health care providers are touting the benefits of vertically integrating regional delivery systems that stress a continuum of care. These integrated delivery systems are achievable through mergers with hospitals, joint ventures or alliances between hospitals and physicians (Anderson 1992). Burns (1994) illustrates how hospitals recognize the power and success behind outpatient centers as the number of the number of ambulatory centers owned and operated by hospitals and independent providers increased 32% in 1993. The trend toward these affiliations between hospitals and networks will expand significantly in the coming years (Burns 1994).

Satellite medical out-patient centers and urgent care centers have established a market that appeals to people that need outpatient care with the ability to associate the name of the center with an equitable name such as a hospital, insurance carrier or other health care entity. This provides the hospital and other health care entities the ability to reach different geographic, age, race and other demographic variables effectively and efficiently.

Free Standing out-patient health centers are reaping huge benefits in this segment of health care. Henderson (1988) shows how freestanding centers are gaining on surgical sites. These free standing outpatient centers are independently owned and are franchised or privately owned by health care providers. Burns (1994) illustrates that independent outpatient center owners increased their share of facilities 57% in 1993. This double digit growth adds to the heat that hospitals must begin to provide adequate care without over prescribing medications and treatment. This segment of the market appeals to unfilled niches in rural communities that most networks miss and overlook (Burns 1994). Lowell-Smith examines the differences between regional and intrametropolitan locations of free standing ambulatory centers and finds that they both serve different demographic consumers and are well developed to address specific needs based on geographic location. Outpatient medical centers

83

have expanded their level of segmentation to include demographic variables as race, age and sex.

Nursing Homes have penetrated the health care market segment that identifies with skilled nursing facilities or long term care facilities. Skilled nursing facilities are broadening their focus to provide services to all people with chronic illnesses and disabilities, not just the elderly. Clearly (1995) reports that the integration of home care, community health services and sub acute care can significantly reduce costs and improve the delivery and quality of health care for everyone. Clearly (1995) further contends that skilled nursing facilities can save Medicare $9 billion dollars a year by providing sub acute services up to 60% cheaper than hospital. Skilled nursing facilities appeal to a segment of patients in the market with chronic illnesses that have limited amounts of coverage. These facilities provide substantial savings that cannot be matched by long-term hospital care. Picard (1988) points to the fact that retirement communities are redesigning their facilities to include campus style environments and skilled nursing facilities.

Long term care that is provided by nursing homes have also taken a new turn following recent Medicare regulations that have opened the door for yet another segment of the health care market. Eubanks (1988) illustrates how Medicare has not included certain chronic conditions necessitating long term custodial care. As a result, new governmental rulings force consumers to attain additional premiums. These long term patients will have to look at other options as ways to medicate and heal. Canning (1993) examines the fact that eldercare is not synonymous with nursing home long-term care. She shows how this opens up new viable markets that are reaching consumers that need the long-term care coverage. Lazzareschi (1993) shows how in-home health care is expected to blossom in the 90s as the industry will adjust to the mobility of elderly that are not suffering from chronic diseases and don't need highly skilled technicians and health care providers.

In-Home care and hospice care, that offer in-home type atmospheres are other options for the consumer these days as costs are being cut on care and comfort and quality of later life is sought. In-home care can be divided into two areas: (1) Intensive and (2) non-intensive. Many physicians are making more house and hospice calls than ever before. This trend is driven by several factors including; the growing demand for reducing convalescing costs by being at home, the increase of primary care doctors that work for health care organizations that are cost conscious, the interest of the medical profession to cater to needs of consumers that want to "heal at home" and Medicare reimbursement for home visits have doubled from about $27.50 cents to approximately $50.00 dollars. Finally, research indicates that by the year 2016, those most likely to need home care will grow to 4.3 million as the population will begin to age at around 85 years old.

Intensive home or hospice care has increased significantly in the past few years as patients have been concerned with living their last days out in the comfort of their own home or homelike environment without adding stress to families with extra costs for caring for them. Greene (1994) provides an illustration of a Florida hospital's effort to satisfy the consumer by agreeing to pay for the home care of a teenager declared to be brain dead. The cost per day for home care was only $1,500 dollars versus $3000 dollars if he were in the hospital.

Non-intensive homecare is a viable option for patients that want to save money and believe that their recovery level will be greatly increased in familiar environment of the home. Lumsdon (1994) shows how homecare services are on the rise where patients are opting to go home and heal even after surgery that traditionally required hospitalization. Now with assisted home care plans, nurses and doctors visit patients and cut cost significantly. Home care can cost 15% of hospital costs and Medicare patients now receive 60-85% of home care services.

The change in the In-home market has provided unique segments of patients who prefer to medicate and convalesce at home. The savings and added comfort of homecare has satisfied a much needed area in health care that will help the industry reduce costs and maximize satisfaction of consumers.

Chapter 9

Segmentation Based on Demographics and Psychographics

Each of the foregoing segments (based on the type of medical care required) can be further segmented based on demographic and psychographic characteristics. For example, demographic information has been used to target the 50 to 64 year old market. This demographic group had been ignored for a long time and now health care providers are developing profitable programs that meet this segment's needs. Burns (1992) shows how health care providers are offering seminars to this age group on self-esteem assertiveness and menopause management. There is also a practical reason for targeting middle aged adults. This group has been found to account for

60% of all health care spending and is expected to increase to 80 million in the 21st century. Likewise, some hospitals are now employing "zip code surgery" as they used demographic information to track surgery incidence within a given area (Schwartz 1988). Zip code databases and their maps and tables are used to track surgery and other medical procedures that take place at a given time of year in various areas across the country. As a result, health care providers can target and design medical coverage based on incidence and effectively plan strategies to reach various consumer segments.

Psychographic segmentation is another way that health care providers can effectively develop and deliver unique services to patients. Benefit segmentation is a popular method of effectively reaching consumers through psychographic probing. John (1992) shows how understanding health care behaviors can improve the strategies of preventive-oriented health care providers. The research shows how there are various benefit driven consumers that exist that define a segmented market that health care providers should tap into.

The benefit segmentation processes consist of psychographic, socioeconomic and role behavior variables that can possibly unlock underlying motives and attitudes that consumers have about health care services. Brown (1992) shows how a benefit segmentation study revealed that a connection exists between attitude toward health care and perceived benefits of fitness. For example, 50% of the sample that regularly exercised produced three groups that shared their perceived benefits of regular exercise. Those groups were : (1) *"the winners"* that will do anything to get ahead in life, (2) *"the dieters"* who will exercise to maintain their appearance and (3) *"the self improvers"* who exercise to feel better. These categories can be used to target and segment groups to help hospitals, fitness centers and other health care providers with information that will help them develop strategies that appeal to various segments that exist.

Once the target consumer segments have been identified, marketing programs must be developed to meet the specific needs of each segment. This involves the formulation of appropriate product management, pricing, promotion, and distribution strategies. These

94

strategies for providing health care effectively and efficiently are considered next.

Conclusion

As marketing orientation and governmental insurance plans become more pronounced and more pervasive in the health care industry, the provision of health care will become more effective and efficient. Consumer health care needs must be more clearly identified and customers targeted more efficiently. Appropriate health care products and services must be developed to meet specific needs. Competitive pricing will emerge, value added advertising and promotional programs implemented, efficient forms of health care delivery will emerge, and accessibility to health services improved. This will go a long way in addressing the health care crisis in the United States. There is reason for this optimism as already we are beginning to see positive results in some sectors of health care. However, it is too soon to declare a victory over health care cost inflation. Fewer Americans, percentagewise, are covered through their employers, and 17 percent of nonelderly Americans are still uninsured . However, with the advent of governmental insurance plans, traditional insurers must restructure their marketing efforts and offerings in order to remain a viable, profitable and sustainable place in the health care industry. Thus, insurers need to keep pressing ahead with a marketing orientation approach in the health care industry. Furthermore, as consumer and marketplace conditions continue to change, the healthcare industry must further specialize in marketing strategies that will cut costs and increase efficiencies. Healthcare providers must segment beyond, basic medical care, hospital stay care, outpatient care, nursing home care and In-home care. They must begin to look at the entire marketing mix variables and the effect those variables will have on segmentation strategies. Consumer relationship marketing strategies utilized through a strong marketing research and information systems focus should prove to provide the cost effectiveness that leads to increased profitability over the long run as they are forced to compete with governmental health plans.

References

Andaleeb, Syed, S. (1994) "Hospital Advertising: The Influence Of Perceptual And   Demographic Factors On Consumer Dispositions," *Hospitals & Health Services Administration,* (Winter), 8, 48-60.

Anders, George (1995) "The HMO Trend: Big, Bigger, Biggest," *The Wall Street Journal,* (March), B1, B4.

Anderson, Howard J. (1992) "Hospitals Seek New Ways To Integrate Health Care," *Hospitals,* 10, (April), 26.

Anderson, Howard J. and Julie Johnsson (1992) "There No Simple Cure For Billing And Pricing Woes," *Hospitals,* 66, (June), 26-34.

Assael, Henry A. (1994) Consumer Behavior & Marketing Action. Cincinnati, Ohio: South-Western College Publishing

Baum, Neil (1992) "Niche Marketing Offers many Opportunities," *American Medical News,* (June), 35, 22-25.

Bazzoli, Fred (1993) "Making The Grade with ER Patients," *Modern Healthcare*, 23, (Dec.), 52-56.

Bergman, Rhonda (1994) "Are Patients Happy?," *Hospitals & Health Networks*, 68, (Dec.), 68-74.

Betts, Mitch (1992) "Make Way For A Better Map: Travelers' Desktop Mapping System Helps Match Doctors and Clients," *Computerworld*, (August), 26, 36.

Blankenau, Renee (1993) "Designing HIPCs," *Hospitals & Health Networks*, (July), 67, 34-36.

Blankenau, Renee (1994) "The Flat Rate Debate," *Hospitals & Health Networks,* 68, (October), 78-80.

Bowers, Michael R and Jack A. Taylor (1990) "Product Line Management in Hospitals: An Exploratory Study Of Managing Change," *Hospitals & Health Services Administration,* (Fall), 365-75.

Braus, Pat (1990) " The Who and Where Of Heart Disease," *Business Week,* (Nov), 12, 32-38.

Braus, Patricia (1993) "Return Of The House Call," *American Demographics,* 15, (March), 24.

Brown, Joseph (1992) "Benefit Segmentation Of The Fitness Market," *Health Marketing Quarterly,* (Summer-Fall), 9, 19-29.

Burns, John (1992) "Health Programs Target
Needs Of Mature Adults," *Modern Healthcare,*
(July), 22, 31.

Burns, John (1994) "Hospitals Splurge On Selling
Efforts," *Modern Healthcare*, (March), 24, 92.

Burns, John (1994) "Outpatient Care Growing
Both In Numbers, Scope," *Modern Healthcare*, 3,
(May), 81.

Business Week editorial (1995) "Managed care
Beats Medicare Any Day," *Business Week,*
(February), 136.

Byrne, Margaret M. "Incentives for Vertical
Integration in Healthcare: The Effect of
Reimbursement Systems/Practitioner Response,"
Journal of Healthcare Marketing, (January), v.44,
43-46.

Caesar, Neil (1996) "The Dangers-and Opportunities-Of a Maturing Health Care Market," *Managed Care,* (February), 50-53.

Canning, JoAnn (1993) "A Guide To New Elder Care Options And Services," National Underwriter Life & Health-Financial Services, (February) 18-20.

Cleary, Allison (1995) "The Long-Term Care," *Hospitals & Health Networks*, 3, (March), 61-63.

Colford, Alice Z. (1994) "Health Ads To Hit Epidemic Level," *Advertising Age*, 65, (July), 42.

Cortez, John P. (1992) "Media Pioneers Try To Corral On-The-Go Consumers," *Advertising Age*, 63, (Aug.), 25.

Denitto, Emily (1994) "Patient Power Over Hospitals, "*Advertising Age*, (Oct.) 65, 46.

Droste, Therese (1988) "Accountability: Direct response helps Marketers," *Hospitals*, 62, (July), 44-46.

Edmondson, Brad (1989) "A Moment on The lips," *American Demographics*, (Dec), 11, 9.

Elgin, Peggie R. (1992) "Companies Band Together To battle healthcare Prices," *Corporate Cashflow Magazine,* (June), 13, 8-10.

Ernst and Whinney (1983) *"Strategic Program Unit Planning: Strategies and Management Tools For A product-Oriented Market Place,"* Chicago: Ernst and Whinney.

Farley, Dean E. (1990) "Case Mix Specialization In The Market Of Hospital Services," *Health Services Research*, (Dec.), 25, 757-784.

Fitzgerald, Kate (1993) "Frankel Prescribes Coupons For Patients," *Advertising Age*, 64, (Oct.), 46.

Flanagan, Patrick (1988) "Emergency Treatment For healthcare Systems," *Computer Decisions,* 20, 43-50.

Flethcher, Meg (1993) "Comp Medical Costs Up, Utilization, Not Pricing, The Reason: Study," *Business Insurance*, (Dec.), 27, 1-2.

Fost, Dan (1992) "U. S. Hospitals Entice Mexicans," *American Demographics*, 14, (Nov), 25.

France, Karen R. and Rajiv Grover (1992) "What Is Healthcare Product?," *Journal Of Healthcare Marketing*, 12, (2), 31-38.

Frenzen, Paul D. (1991) "The Increasing Supply Of Physicians In US Urban and Rural Areas," *Business Week*, (Sept.), 81, 1141-1148.

Gattuso, Greg (1994) "New Infomercial For St. Jude's Hospital," *Fund Raising Management*, 25, (March), 12.

Gehrt, Kenneth C. and Mary Beth Pinto (1993) "Assessing the Availability Of Situationally Driven Segmentation Opportunities, *Health Services Administration*, (Summer), 38, 243-266.

Goodwin, Michael (1994) "Doctor On A Disc," *PC World*, 12, (June), 315-317.

Gorchels, Linda M. (1995) "Traditional Product Management Evolves," *Marketing News*, (Jan. 30), 29, 4.

Gould, Stephen J. (1988) "Consumer Attitudes Toward health and Healthcare," *Journal Of Consumer Affairs,* (Summer), 22, 96-119.

Grayson, Mary (1994) "1994: Going Beyond Reform," *Hospitals & Health Networks,* (Jan.), 68, 6.

Garzier, Kyle L. (1999) "Collaboration and Quality in Managed Care," *Journal of Healthcare Management,* (May), v.44, 163-165.

Greene, Jay (1994) "Hospitals To Pay For Care At Home For Teen In Coma," *Modern Healthcare,* 24, (April), 34.

Greene, Jay (1995) "Emergency Firm Links With Hospitals," *Modern Healthcare,* 25, (Feb.) 36.

Guseman, Patricia K. (1988) "How To Pick The Best Location," *American Demographics,* (Aug.), 10, 42-44.

Haggerty, Alfred C. (1993) "New Mega-Managed Care Co. In California," *National Underwriter Life & Health-Financial Services,* (July), 3-5.

Hamel, Ruth and Tim Schreiner (1988) "Selling Splinters To Skiers," *American Demographics*, 10, (Oct.), 54.

Hariton, Theodore (1998) "A New Model For Health Care," *Managed Care,* (Dec.), 80-84.

Henderson, John A. (1988) "Freestanding Centers Gaining On Surgical Suites," *Modern Healthcare,* 4 (June), 84.

Hiestand, Michael (1988) "Hospital Offers Coupons For Free Clinic Tests," *Adweek*, 29, (October), 34.

Investor's Business Daily editorial (1995) "What about Healthcare," *Investor's Business Daily*, (February), A2.

John, Judy (1992) "A Model For Understanding Benefit Segmentation I Preventive Healthcare," *Healthcare Management Review,* 17, 21-31.

Johnsson, Julie (1992) "Image Obsession: Is It healthy For CEOs?," *Hospitals,* (Aug.), 66, 56.

Keehan, S. et al. (2008) "health Spending Projections Through 2017," *Health Affairs Web Exclusive*, (February), w 146:21

Kenkel, Paul J. (1993) "Human, Principal health Expand Into New Markets Through Acquisition Deals," *Modern Healthcare,* 23, 6.

King, Brent (1993) "Public Relations Fund Raising And Marketing In Canadian Hospitals: The Potential For Encroachment," *Public Relations Quarterly,* (Summer), 38, 40-46.

Laderman, Jeffrey (1995) "This HMO Should Get Well Soon," *Business Week,* (March), 112.

Lau, Gloria (1995) "Controlling Healthcare Costs For Self-Insured" (1995) *Investors' Business Daily,* (April), A6.

Lau, Gloria (1995) "More Lucrative Medicare Market," (1995) *Investors' Business Daily,* (April), A6.

Lowell-Smith, Elizabeth G. (1993) "Regional and Intrametropolitan Differences In The Location Of Free Standing Ambulatory Surgery Centers," *The Professional Geographer*, 10, (November), 398-399.

Lumsdon, Kevin (1992) "Smart Moves: Good Management, Not Technology, Will Steer Movement To Outpatient Care," *Hospitals*, 2 (Oct.), 18.

Lumsdon, Kevin (1994) "No Place Like Home," *Hospitals & Health Networks*, 68, (Oct.), 44-50.

Lutz, Sandy (1994) "Ambulance Companies The Latest Target Of Mergers, Acquisitions," *Modern Healthcare*, (May) 24, 93-95.

Malhotra, Naresh K. (1986a), "Market Segmentation and Strategic Growth Opportunities for Hospitals," *Journal of Health Care Marketing*, Vol. 6, No. 2, 2-6.

113

Malhotra, Naresh K. (1986b), "Hospital Marketing In The Changing Health Care Environment," *Journal Of Healthcare Marketing*, (Sept.), 6, (3) 37-48.

Malhotra, Naresh K. (1988), "Health Care Marketing Warfare," *Journal of Health Care Marketing*, Vol. 8, No. 1, March 1988, 17-29.

Malhotra, Naresh K. (1996), *Marketing Research: An Applied Orientation*, Second Edition, Upper Saddle River, NJ: Prentice Hall, Inc.

Munro, Dan (2012), U. S, Healthcare Hits $3 Trillion Dollars, *Forbes*, January.

McNamee, Mike (1995) "Give Medicare A Strong Dose Of Managed Care," *Business Week*, (February), 44.

MCOL (2012) Current HMO enrollment report, http://www.mcol.com/current_enrollment.

Menduno, Michael (1999) "Net Profits," *Hospitals & Health Networks*, (V.73) 44-50.

Merline, John (1995) "Shortcomings of Managed Care," *Investors Business Daily,* (March), A1, A2.

Miller, Andy (1995) "Healthcare Treated In A New Way," *Atlanta Journal Constitution*, (February), H1.

Miller, Andy (1996) "Health Benefits Cost Employers Just 2.1% More in '95, Survey Says," *Atlanta Journal Constitution*, (January), D3.

Modern healthcare Editorial (1993) "Giant Merger Is Latest Offshoot Of Managed Care, Reform trend," *Modern Healthcare,* (Oct.), 33.

Myerson, Allen R. (1995) "Helping Health Insurers Say No," The New York Times, (March), C1, C3.

Nackel, John G. and Irvin W. Kues (1987)
"Product Line Management: Systems and
Strategies," *Hospitals and Health Services
Administration*, (March-April), 109-23.

Naidu, G. M., Arno Kleimenhagen and George D.
Pillari (1993) "Is Product Line Management
Appropriate For Your Healthcare Facility,"
Journal Of Healthcare Marketing, (Fall), 13, (3),
6-17.

Nemes, Judith (1993) "For Profit Hospitals
Waving Goodbye To Era Of High Prices,"
Hospitals & Health Networks, (March), 23, 33-41.

Peltier, James W. (1994) "Taking The Route: To
Enhance Awareness And Image, Many Hospitals
Today Are Passing Up Traditional Advertising In
favor Of Direct Marketing Strategies," *Journal Of
Healthcare Marketing*, 14, (Fall), 22-28.

Perry, Linda (1988) "Despite Revamped Mail rates, Savings Can Be Posted," *Modern Healthcare,* 18, (April) 42.

Perry, Linda (1989) "Memorial health $2 million dollar Campaign Touts New Image," *Modern Healthcare*, 19, (June), 85.

Perry, Linda (1991) "Hospital Groups Turning To Adversarial Campaigns To Improve Public Image," *Modern Healthcare* 21, (Feb.), 24-28.

Petrecca, Laura (1999) "WebMD's $25 Million Dollar Campaign Touts Intelligent Wit," *Advertising Age,* (v.70) 42.

Picard, Maureen (1988) "Inn Thing: This Attractive Campus Style Community For Active Seniors Also Offers A Skilled Nursing Facility," *Restaurant Hotel Design International,* 10, 38-44.

Rabinowitz, Allen (1992) "Colby Goes Over The Rainbow For Hospital Spots," *Back Stage-Shoot*, 33, 8-10.

Raphael, Steve (1993) "Hospital Marketing Targets Doctors, Consumers," *Crain's Detroit Business,* 9, (Aug.), 13.

Reddy, Allen C. (1993) "Positioning Hospitals: A Model For Regional Hospitals," *Journal Of Healthcare Marketing*, (Winter) 13, 40-45.

Ristino, Robert J. (1989) "Public Relations Marketing," *Healthcare Management Review*, 14, (Spring), 79-86.

Rosenberg, Hilary (1995) "Surgery For Healthcare Products," *Institutional Investor*, (Feb.), 29, 23-25.

Rosenfield, James R. (1994) "In The Mail," *Direct Marketing*, 57, (Oct.), 57, 30-33.

Rosenthal, Elisabeth (1995) "H. M. O.'s On The Rise in New York," *New York Times*, (March), A1.

Rosko, Michal D. (1994) Hospital Markups: Responses To Environmental Pressures In Pennsylvania," *Hospital & Health Services Administration*, (Spring), 39, 3-17.

Schiffman, Leon G. and Leslie L. Kanuk (1994) Consumer Behavior, Englewood Cliffs, New Jersey: Prentice Hall.

Schlossberg, Howard (1990) "Healthcare Looks For Hero In Marketing," *Marketing News*, (Jan.), 24, 1-3.

Schwartz, Joe (1988) "Zip Code Surgery," *American Demographics*, (Nov), 10, 48.

Schwartz, Joe (1994) "Improving Economic Incentives In Hospital Perspective Payment Systems Through Equilibrium Pricing," Management Science, (June) 40, 774-788.

Sherrid, Pamela (1999) "What's Up Doc?" US News and World Report, (v.126), 60.

Silberner, Joanne (1997) "In The Shadow of The Managed care Monolith," *Business and Health,* 30-33.

Stodghill II, Ron , Eric Schine and Joseph Weber (1995) "Sudden Illness," *Business Week,* (May), 32-33.

Sturm, Arthur C. (1988) "Innovative Advertising Becoming Vital In An Increasingly Competitive Market," *Modern Healthcare,* 18, (June), 33.

Taylor, Kathryn (1993) How Feuding Hospitals Joined Forces To Serve Their Community," *Hospitals & Health Networks,* (Dec.), 67, 10.

Taylor, Kathryn S. (1994) "Changing Course: Realigning The Supply Chain," *Hospitals & Networks,* 68, (April), 28-34.

The Henry J. Kaiser family Foundation (2008) *"Employee Health Benefits: 2008 Annual Survey"*, (September 2008).

Thomas, Richard K. (1993) "What Hospitals Must Do," American Demographics, 15, (Jan.), 36-41.

Wagner, Mary (1992) "Hospital campaign Against Drug Price Increase Is Making A Dent," *Modern Healthcare*, (March), 22, 30.

West, Betsy (1995) "Reorganizing The laboratory To better Serve Patients," *Medical Laboratory Observer*, 27, (Feb.), 51-58.

Williams, Melony (1994) "Capital Acquisition Planning In A Managed Care Environment," *Health Management Technology*, (Nov), 15, 20.

Zelman, William N. and Curtis P McLaughlin (1990) "Product Lines in a Complex Marketplace:

Matching Organizational Strategy to Buyer Behavior," *Healthcare Management Review*, 15 (2), 9-14.

For Speaking Engagements

admin@newzionchristianchurch.org or

678.845.7055

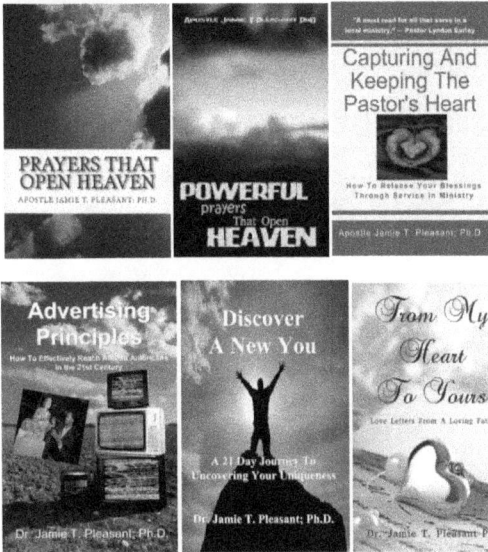

These books can be purchased at any bookstore or online at amazon.com, barnesandnoble.com and many other stores and outlets.

About the Author

Dr. Jamie T. Pleasant; Ph.D. is a tenured marketing professor at Clark Atlanta University, which is an AACSB accredited institution of higher learning. AACSB accreditation is the highest and most distinguished accredited affiliation of business schools around the entire world. He is also the Chief Executive Pastor and Founder of New Zion Christian Church in Suwanee, Georgia. As a modern day polymath, he holds a bachelor's degree in Physics from Benedict College in Columbia, South Carolina, Marketing Studies from Clemson University and an M.B.A. in Marketing from Clark Atlanta University. On August 13, 1999, Apostle Pleasant achieved a Georgia Tech milestone by becoming the first African American to graduate with a Ph.D. in Business Management in the school's 120 plus year history.

God gave him the vision to establish a Biblically based economic development initiative for New Zion Christian Church. He remains at the pulse of the economic business sector. As a result, Apostle Pleasant is in constant demand to train, speak and teach others at all levels in ministries and the private sector about business and economic development across the country. He has created cutting edge and industry leading ministerial programs in the church such as The Financial Literacy Academy For Youth (FLAFY), where youth from the ages of 13-19 attend 12 week intense classes on financial money management principles. At the end of 12 weeks, they receive a "Personal Finance" certificate of achievement. Other ministries he has pioneered include; The Wealth Builders Investment Club (WBIC), which educates and allows members to actively invest in the stock market, along with the much celebrated Institute of Entrepreneurship (IOE), where participants earn a certificate in

Entrepreneurship after three months of comprehensive training in all aspects of starting and owning a successful competitive business. The main goal and purpose of IOE is that each year one of the trained businesses will be awarded up to $10,000 start up money to ensure financial success. The newly added SAT & PSAT prep courses for children ages 9-19 fuels the potential success of all who walk through the doors of New Zion Christian Church.

Apostle Pleasant has met with political officials such as President Clinton and Nelson Mandela. He has delivered the opening prayer for the born again Christian and comedian, Steve Harvey. He has performed marriage ceremonies and counseled numerous celebrated personalities such as Usher Raymond (Confessions Recording Artist), Terri Vaughn (Lavita Jenkins on The Steve Harvey Show), and many others.

He is civically engaged as well. After the Columbine High School shooting, he founded the

National School Safety Advocacy Association. His latest foundations include the Young Entrepreneurship Program (YEP) and the African American Consumer Economic Rights (AACER).

He has authored eight books, *Prayers That Open Heaven, Capturing and Keeping the Pastor's Heart, Powerful Prayers That Open Heaven, Advertising Principles: How to Effectively Reach African Americans in the 21st Century, Discover a New You: A 21 Day Journey to Uncovering Your Uniqueness, From My Heart To Yours: Love Letters From A Loving Father, Today's Apostle: Servants of God, Leading His People towards Unity and An Overview of Strategic Health Marketing: Marketing Mix and Segmentation Strategies at Work*.

Dr. Pleasant is the husband of Kimberly Pleasant (whom he loves dearly) and the proud father of three children: Christian, Zion and Nacara.

FINI